W9-BHL-632

Far-Out Science Projects About Earth's
Sun and Moon

ROBERT GARDNER

ILLUSTRATIONS BY TOM LABAFF

Enslow Elementary

an imprint of

Enslow Publishers, Inc.

40 Industrial Road
Box 398
Berkeley Heights, NJ 07922
USA

http://www.enslow.com

Enslow Elementary, an imprint of Enslow Publishers, Inc.

Enslow Elementary® is a registered trademark of Enslow Publishers, Inc.

Library of Congress Cataloging-in-Publication Data

Gardner, Robert, 1929–
    Far-out science projects about Earth's sun and moon / Robert Gardner.
        p. cm. — (Rockin' Earth science experiments)
    Includes bibliographical references and index.
    ISBN-13: 978-0-7660-2736-7
    ISBN-10: 0-7660-2736-8
    1. Sun—Experiments—Juvenile literature. 2. Moon—Experiments—Juvenile literature. 3. Science projects—Juvenile literature. I. Title. II. Series: Gardner, Robert, 1929–   Rockin' Earth science experiments.
    QB521.5.G368 2007
    523.7078—dc22

                              2006013789

Printed in the United States of America

10 9 8 7 6 5 4 3 2 1

To Our Readers: We have done our best to make sure all Internet Addresses in this book were active and appropriate when we went to press. However, the author and the publisher have no control over and assume no liability for the material available on those Internet sites or on other Web sites they may link to. Any comments or suggestions can be sent by e-mail to comments@enslow.com or to the address on the back cover.

Illustration credits: Tom LaBaff

Photo credits: Colin Cuthbert/Photo Researchers, Inc., p. 12; Dept of Physics, Imperial College/ Photo Researchers, Inc., p. 28; John W. Bova/Photo Researchers, Inc., p. 44; NASA Glenn Research Center, p. 33; NASA Kennedy Space Center, p. 36; NASA Marshall Space Flight Center, pp. 40, 41; Shutterstock.com, pp. 9, 20; Simon Fraser/Photo Researchers, Inc., pp. 16, 25.

Cover photo: Detlev van Ravenswaay/Photo Researchers, Inc.

Contents

Experiments with a 🎗 symbol feature **Ideas for Your Science Fair.**

Introduction

The sun and Earth are very far apart from each other—93 million miles! Yet they are joined by a special force. That force is gravity. The sun's gravity makes Earth move around the sun. We say Earth orbits the sun. How lucky for us! The sun gives us the light and heat we need to live.

In the same way, Earth's gravity makes the moon move around us. Sometimes you see a bright moon at night. Other times, even if the sky is clear, you can't see the moon at night. You will find out why as you do the experiments in this book. You will also learn a lot more about both the sun and the moon.

Entering a Science Fair

Most of the experiments in this book have ideas for science fair projects. However, judges at science fairs like experiments that are creative, so do not simply copy an experiment from this book. Pick one of the ideas and develop a project of your own. Choose something you really like and want to know more about. It will be more interesting to you. And it can lead to a creative experiment that you plan and carry out.

Before entering a science fair, read one or more of the books listed under Further Reading. They will give you helpful hints and lots of useful information about science fairs.

Safety First

To do experiments safely, always follow these rules:

1 Never look at the sun. It can cause permanent damage to your eyes!

2 Always do experiments under adult supervision.

3 Read all instructions carefully. If you have questions, check with the adult.

4 Be serious when experimenting. Fooling around can be dangerous to you and to others.

5 Keep the area where you work clean and organized. When you have finished, clean up and put all of your materials away.

6 Use only alcohol thermometers. Some thermometers contain liquid mercury. It is dangerous to touch or breathe mercury vapors. Mercury thermometers have been banned in many states. If you have a mercury thermometer in your house, ask an adult if it can be taken to a local mercury thermometer exchange location.

Getting Direction from the Sun

How can you use the sun to find out which way is north? Write down your ideas and your reasons for them.

Now Let's Find Out!

Ask **an adult** to help you with this experiment. **And remember, do not look directly at the sun! It can damage your eyes!**

1 On a sunny morning, hammer a stake into the ground. Choose a place that is level and will be in the sun all day. Be sure the stake is straight up and down.

2 A bit before midday (11 A.M. to 1 P.M.) begin marking the end of the stake's shadow every 5 or 10 minutes. You can use a stick to make a scratch mark, or you can mark the positions with Popsicle sticks. Keep doing this until you

can see that the shadow is getting longer.

ends of longer, earlier shadows

end of shortest shadow

where shadow is now

3 Use a yardstick or tape measure to find the length of the shadows you marked. Find the mark where the stake's shadow was shortest. That shadow pointed north. Hammer a second stake into the ground on that mark.

A line connecting the first stake with the second points north. A line from the second stake to the first points south.

4 How can you find east and west? Leave the stakes in the ground for more experiments.

measuring the shortest shadow

Getting Direction from the Sun
An Explanation

The sun reaches its highest point in the sky at midday. It casts the shortest shadows at that time. Midday (the time halfway between sunrise and sunset) may not be at noon. At midday, the sun is directly above a point south of you. It casts a shadow that points north.

To find east and west, stand in front of

1st stake

2nd stake

the first stake. Face north. Raise your arms straight out. Your right arm will point to the east. Your left arm will point to the west.

FACT: Shadows seen in photographs taken from an airplane can sometimes reveal the shapes of the objects casting the shadows.

Ideas for Your Science Fair

- Does midday where you live always happen at the same time? Do experiments to find out.

- Use a globe and a soda straw to find out where the sun is directly overhead at midday.

Sunrise, Sunset, and Season

It will take a year to do Experiments 2 and 3, but you can learn a lot from them. While doing these two experiments, you can do Experiments 4 through 10.

As you will see, the sun follows a path across the sky. Do you think its path will begin (sunrise) and end (sunset) in the same places as the seasons change? Write down your ideas and your reasons for them.

THINGS YOU WILL NEED:
- clock or watch
- stakes from Experiment 1 to find true east
- paper and pencil
- calendar

Now Let's Find Out!

1   Get up in time to see the sun rise. Use the stakes from Experiment 1 to find east. Standing between those stakes, note the direction of sunrise. **Do not look directly into the sun!**

2   Draw a diagram like the one shown. On your diagram, write something to help you remember where the sun rose.

You might write, "Just left of the Smith's garage," "Behind our big maple tree," or something like that. Don't forget to date your diagram.

Did the sun rise north of east? South of east? Or true east (in line with your location of east in Experiment 1)?

3 Do the same thing from the same place at sunset.

4 Continue to mark the direction to sunrise and sunset at least once a month for a year. Be sure you always stand on the same spot, between the same two stakes. What changes do you think you will see?

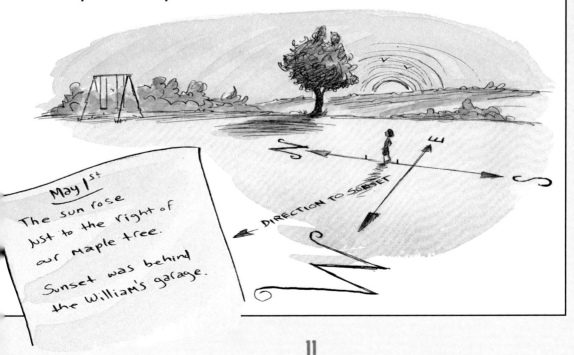

May 1st
The sun rose just to the right of our maple tree.
Sunset was behind the William's garage.

DIRECTION TO SUNSET

Sunrise, Sunset, and Season
An Explanation

As you have probably discovered, the sun does not always rise in the same place. It does not always set in the same place either. In the northern hemisphere, from spring through summer, the sun rises and sets north of east. In the fall and winter, it rises and sets south of east. A true east sunrise and a true west sunset happen only twice a year. Those dates are the first day of spring (around March 21) and the first day of fall (around September 21). On those two days, the sun shines directly on Earth's equator.

FACT: Architects who build solar-heated buildings must consider the locations of sunrise and sunset.

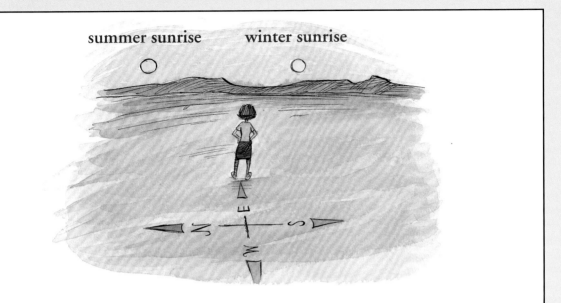

summer sunrise   winter sunrise

Ideas for Your Science Fair 🎀

- Use shadows to show the direction of sunrise and sunset.

- Record the time of sunrise and the time of sunset as seasons pass. How can you explain these time changes?

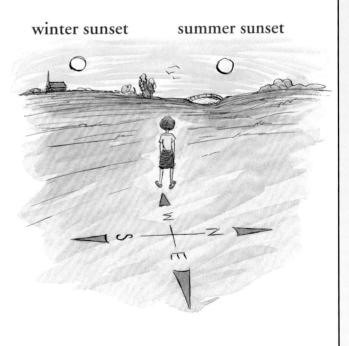

winter sunset   summer sunset

3

Seasons and the Midday Sun

How does the height of the sun's path across the sky change as seasons pass? Write down your ideas and your reasons for them.

Now Let's Find Out!

Shadows can be used to compare the height of any light, including the sun. You can do an experiment to see that this is true.

THINGS YOU WILL NEED:
- pencil
- clay
- sheet of paper
- dark room
- flashlight
- stake from Experiment 1
- yardstick
- pencil
- notebook

1   Stick a pencil upright in a small lump of clay. Put the pencil and clay on a sheet of paper on the floor.

2   Turn out the lights so the room is dark.

3   Shine a flashlight on the pencil. Watch its shadow as you move the flashlight higher. Watch its shadow as you lower the flashlight. When is the shadow longest? When is it shortest?

4 Go to the first stake you put in the ground during Experiment 1. Mark the ends of its shadows around midday. Write down the length of its shortest (midday) shadow in a notebook.

5 Continue to measure its shortest midday shadow at different times of the year. What do your measurements tell you about the sun's height during its path across the sky? How does the height of its path change as the seasons pass?

Seasons and the Midday Sun
An Explanation

As you found, the pencil's shadow grew longer when the flashlight was held lower. The shadow grew shorter as you shined the light from a higher place.

The same is true of shadows cast by the sun. A midday summer sun casts short shadows. The midday winter sun's shadows are much longer. The path of a summer sun is high and long. The path of a winter sun is shorter and lower. Compare the time for the sun to travel across summer and winter skies. Which path takes longer?

FACT: The summer sun never sets at the North Pole. Meanwhile, the winter sun never rises at the South Pole.

Midnight sun over Greenland (North Pole area).

Ideas for Your Science Fair

- Use a clear plastic dome to represent the sky. Figure out a way to map the sun's path across the sky on the dome.

- On a sunny day, how does the length and direction of your shadow change? Can you explain the changes you see?

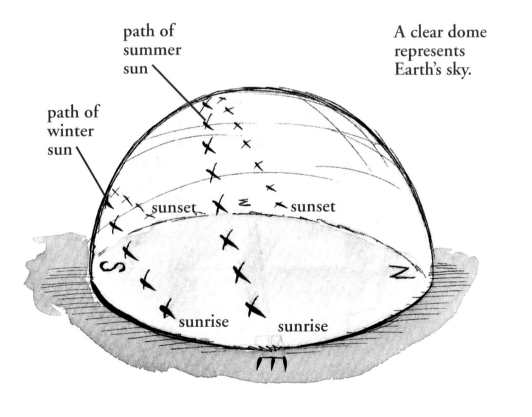

path of summer sun

A clear dome represents Earth's sky.

path of winter sun

sunset

sunset

sunrise

sunrise

Getting Time from the Sun

How can you use the sun to make a clock? Write down or draw your ideas and your reasons for them.

4

THINGS YOU WILL NEED:

- board at least 12 in (30 cm) on each side
- tape
- sheet of paper
- hammer
- finishing nail 2–3 in (5–8 cm) long
- sunny, level place outdoors
- chalk
- pencil
- watch or clock

Now Let's Find Out!

1 Find a board at least 12 inches (30 centimeters) square. Tape a sheet of paper to the board. Hammer a finishing nail a short way into the board. The nail should be upright and near one end of the board as shown.

2 Put the board on a sunny, level place outdoors shortly after sunrise. The nail should be on the south end of the board.

3 Use a pencil to mark the nail's shadow on the paper. Do this every hour until

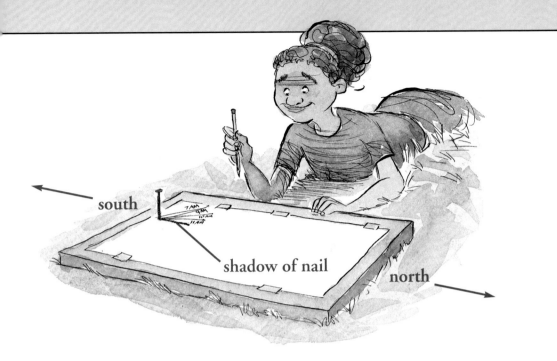

south

shadow of nail

north

sunset. Label each shadow you mark with the time you read on a watch or clock.

4 Use chalk or some other way to mark the outline of the board on the ground so you can put it back in the same place later.

5 After several days, compare the times on your sun clock with the times on your watch or clock. Do the times still agree? Do they agree after a week? After a month? After several months?

Getting Time from the Sun
An Explanation

Early Egyptians used a sun clock like the one you made. As you found, the sun clock is not very accurate. Its time did not agree with your watch or clock time for long. One reason is that Earth's orbit around the sun is an ellipse. An ellipse is an oval shape. In January, when Earth is closest to the sun, it moves faster along its orbit. In July, when it is farther from the sun, it moves slower.

FACT: This clock, called a sundial, can be used to measure time. Its shadow falls across the dial. The device that casts the shadow is called a gnomon. The angle the gnomon makes with the base should equal the latitude of its location.

On a globe you will find an analemma. It looks like a long thin number 8. It shows how much sun time is ahead or behind a clock's time each day of the year.

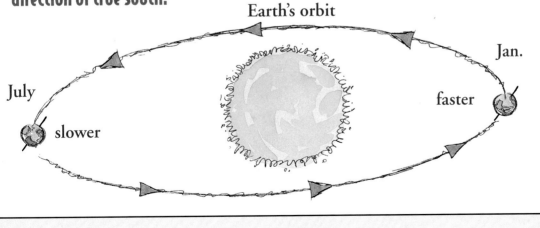

20 10   10 20

minutes ahead of clock

minutes behind clock

Ideas for Your Science Fair

- Build a sundial using a gnomon. The angle (steepness) of the gnomon should match your latitude. Is it a more accurate timer than the sun clock you made?

- Figure out a way to use your watch and the sun to find the approximate direction of true south.

Earth's orbit

Jan.

July

faster

slower

5

Heat from the Sun

Do you think a black surface will take in more of the sun's heat than a silver one? Write down your ideas and your reasons for them.

THINGS YOU WILL NEED:

- 2 aluminum pie pans
- flat black paint
- masking tape
- 2 outdoor alcohol thermometers
- 2 clear plastic bags
- twist ties (if needed to seal bags)
- cardboard box
- window in bright sunlight
- clock or watch

Now Let's Find Out!

1 Get two aluminum pie pans. Paint the inside of one pan with flat black paint. Let the paint dry.

2 Use masking tape to attach an outdoor alcohol thermometer to the inside of each pan. (See the drawing.) Be sure the tape covers the thermometer bulbs.

3 Put each pan inside a clear plastic bag. Seal the bags.

4 Put both pans in a cardboard box. Put the box near a window in bright sunlight. Place the box so that the sun shines directly on both pans.

5 Look at the thermometers every 5 minutes. Does the air temperature inside the pans increase? If it does, in which pan does the air get warmer?

6 Take the pans out of the sunlight before the temperature gets to 100 degrees Fahrenheit (40 degrees Celsius).

Heat from the Sun
An Explanation

Have you ever stood in the bright sun wearing dark clothes? If you have, you may have noticed how warm you felt.

Dark surfaces absorb (take in) more heat from the sun than lighter ones. Lighter surfaces, such as a shiny aluminum pie pan, reflect a lot of the sunlight. The heat in that sunlight is not absorbed. As a result, light-colored things do not get as warm as darker ones.

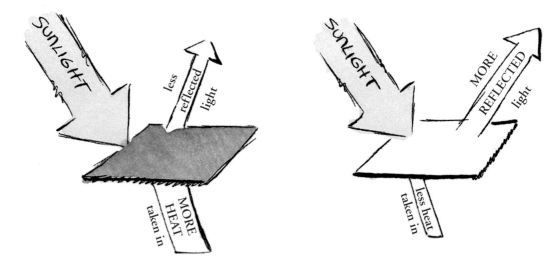

Lots of sunlight is absorbed as heat.　　　Lots of sunlight is reflected.

FACT: Solar collectors like these can be used to change sunlight to heat. The heat can warm both water and air. A building can get room air heat and hot water from the sun.

Solar water heaters in Greece.

Ideas for Your Science Fair 🎀

- Do an experiment to show that you can heat water with sunlight.

- Build a model solar heater from a shoe box.

The Colors in Sunlight

Do you think you can find colors in sunlight? Write down your ideas and your reasons for them.

Now Let's Find Out!

1 Stand with your back to the sun. Use a garden hose with a nozzle to spray a fine mist into the air. The spray should be in front of you as shown in the drawing. What colors do you see? You have made a rainbow. The rainbow shows you all the colors that are in sunlight.

2 Repeat the experiment on a cloudy day when the sun is not shining. Can you see a rainbow? What does this tell you?

3 Here's another way to see what colors are hidden in the sun's light. Hold a prism in

THINGS YOU WILL NEED:
- bright sunshine
- garden hose with spray nozzle
- cloudy day
- prism
- white wall
- lightbulb

sunlight. Hold it near a white wall. Turn the prism until you see a band of colors on the wall.

4 Hold the prism near a white surface several feet from a glowing lightbulb. Can you separate the light from the bulb into colors?

The Colors in Sunlight
An Explanation

A prism can separate ordinary white light into colors. It does this by bending the light. Some colors, such as violet, bend more than others, such as red. The bending makes the white light break apart into all the colors you see in a rainbow.

Raindrops, or water drops sprayed from a hose, act like tiny prisms. They reflect the light and bend it. The bending causes the colors to separate. The reflection sends the colored light back to your eye.

FACT: A spectroscope can separate light into the colors it contains. An element, such as hydrogen, can be energized. Then it gives off colors that can be used to identify it.

These lines are a "fingerprint" for hydrogen.

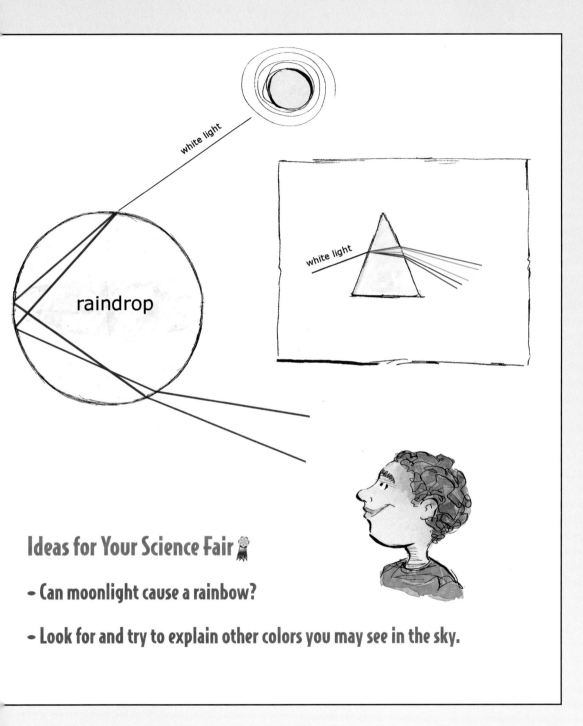

white light

white light

raindrop

Ideas for Your Science Fair

- Can moonlight cause a rainbow?

- Look for and try to explain other colors you may see in the sky.

The Ever-Changing Moon

Does the moon always look the same? If not, does it change from day to day? Write down your ideas and your reasons for them.

Now Let's Find Out!

1 Find your newspaper's weather section. It will tell you the date of a new moon.

2 A day or two after a new moon, look for the moon in the west as the sun sets. What does the moon look like? It is called a crescent moon.

3 Look for the moon each day. Draw pictures of the moon so you will remember its shape. Be sure to look for the moon at sunset. How does its shape change as days pass? How does it appear to move farther from the sun? Where do you see the sun when you see a full moon rising?

4 Because of cloudy weather, you may not see the moon every day. But keep looking for the moon as days and months pass.

THINGS YOU WILL NEED:
- pen or pencil and a notebook
- local newspaper

5 After you see a full moon, begin looking for the moon early in the morning. How does its shape change as days pass? How much time separates one new moon from the next? Why can't you see a new moon?

The Ever-Changing Moon
An Explanation

There are 29 ½ days between new moons. The same time passes between full moons.

You saw a thin crescent moon near the setting sun. The moon grew fatter as it moved farther from the sun in the sky every night. When a full moon is rising, the sun on the opposite side of the sky is setting. After a full moon, you can see the moon in the morning. It shrinks as it slowly moves closer to the sun in the sky. Finally, it becomes a crescent on its other side as it rises shortly before the sun. A new moon

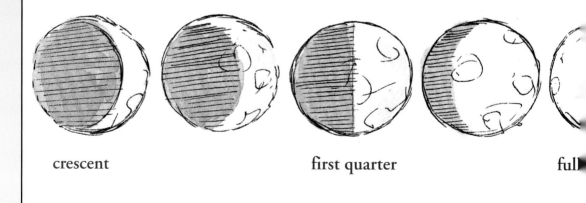

crescent   first quarter   full can't be seen. You will learn why when you do the next experiment.

Ideas for Your Science Fair

- Does the moon always rise in the same place? Does it always set in the same place?

- Why can we sometimes see the moon in the daytime? Why are we sometimes unable to see the moon—even on a clear night?

When astronauts were on the moon and looked toward Earth, this is what they saw.

"Earthrise" as seen from the moon.

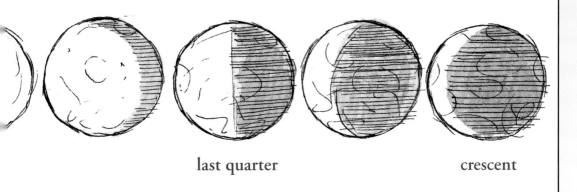

last quarter   crescent

A Moon Model

8

THINGS YOU WILL NEED:

- white Styrofoam ball, white golf ball, or Ping-Pong ball
- long pin or nail or some clay and a stick
- dark room
- incandescent, frosted lightbulb
- stool

Why does the moon's appearance change? Write down your ideas and your reasons for them.

Now Let's Find Out!

1 Put a white Styrofoam ball on the sharp end of a long pin or a nail. (You can also use a white golf ball or a Ping-Pong ball supported by some clay on the end of a stick.) The white ball represents the moon.

2 Do this experiment in a dark room. Turn on one incandescent, frosted lightbulb. The lightbulb represents the sun. Sit on a stool several feet from the lightbulb. Hold the ball above your head. Your head represents Earth.

3 Slowly turn around on the stool, moving to your left. Watch the ball as you turn. Notice how the lighted

(brighter) part of the ball changes. (The darker part of the ball will not be totally dark. Walls and ceiling reflect some light onto the ball). When do you see a crescent moon? A first quarter? A full moon? A last quarter? Another crescent? A new moon?

How does this model help you explain why the appearance of the moon changes? Keep your moon model for Experiment 10.

"sun"

"moon"

You are "Earth."

A Moon Model
An Explanation

As the moon circles around (orbits) Earth, it reflects different amounts of sunlight back to Earth. When it is between Earth and the sun (a new moon), we can't see it. All its reflected light goes back toward the sun. When it is on the side of Earth opposite the sun, we see a full moon. Then the whole side of the moon facing Earth reflects light to us. Between new and full moons, we see different amounts of the moon. You saw how this works as you turned on the stool.

FACT: There is no air on the moon. Astronauts on the moon had to wear special suits and carry oxygen to breathe.

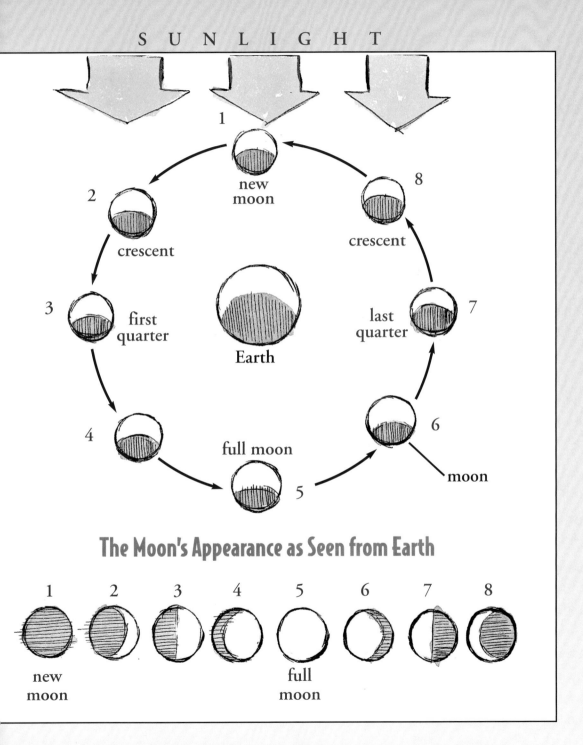

SUNLIGHT

new
moon

crescent

first
quarter

Earth

full moon

moon

last
quarter

crescent

The Moon's Appearance as Seen from Earth

1   2   3   4   5   6   7   8

new
moon

full
moon

9

A Closer Look at the Moon

How will the moon look different if you look at it through binoculars or a telescope? Write down your ideas and your reasons for them.

Now Let's Find Out!

1 Pick a clear night when the moon can be seen. Look at the moon through binoculars or a telescope. Does it look the same as it did when seen with just your eyes? If not, how is it different?

2 Look at the moon through binoculars or a telescope when it is at or near first quarter. Notice the shadows you can see on the moon. What do you think

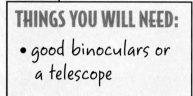

THINGS YOU WILL NEED:
- good binoculars or a telescope

causes the shadows? Where are the shadows longest? Where are they shortest? Why are some shadows longer than others?

A Closer Look at the Moon
An Explanation

Seen through binoculars, the moon is not smooth. It has many "scars" (craters) where meteoroids have hit its surface.

Sunlight makes shadows on the moon just as it does on the earth. The higher the sun, as seen from the moon, the shorter the shadows. The lower the sun, as seen from the moon, the longer the shadows. If you were standing near long shadows on the moon, the sun would be rising or setting. If the shadows were short, the sun would be higher.

FACT: We always see the same side of the moon because the moon turns on its axis at the same rate that it orbits Earth. But we now know what the backside of the moon looks like. While circling the moon, astronauts took photographs of the side that we never see.

The photograph shows the moon at first quarter as seen through a telescope.

Ideas for Your Science Fair

- Look at a full moon when it is rising over the eastern horizon. Then look at it later when it is high in the sky. When does it look larger? Design an experiment to show that its size does not change.

- Try to explain why the moon looks larger as it rises.

10

Eclipses

Sometimes all or part of the sun or moon becomes dark. This is called an eclipse. What causes an eclipse? Write down your ideas and your reasons for them.

Suppose the moon got directly on a line between Earth and the sun. What would happen? (Usually, a new moon is slightly above or below a straight line between Earth and Sun.)

THINGS YOU WILL NEED:

- scissors
- drinking straw
- penny or dime
- frosted lightbulb
- large ball, such as a soccer ball or volleyball
- moon model from Experiment 8

Now Let's Find Out!

1 Use scissors to make a slit in the end of a drinking straw. Put a penny or a dime in the slit.

2 Let a bright, frosted lightbulb represent the sun. The coin represents the moon. Close one eye. Hold the coin close to the other eye. Move the coin between your eye and

the lightbulb. How much of the bulb is covered? How much of it can you see?

3 Move the coin closer to and farther from your eye. Where is the coin when it covers the whole lightbulb? Part of the lightbulb?

4 What happens when the moon blocks the sun from sight? Hold your moon model from Experiment 8 between the lightbulb (sun) and a larger ball (Earth). Look for the smaller ball's (moon's) shadow on the larger ball (Earth).

If you were in the shadow, what would happen to your view of the sun?

Eclipses
An Explanation

Once in a while, the moon passes directly between the sun and Earth. This is called a solar eclipse. When

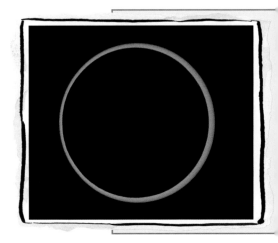

it happens, the moon's shadow falls on Earth. If you are in the dark part of the shadow (see the drawing), the whole sun disappears. If you are in the lighter part of the shadow, part of the sun disappears. **Never look at the sun during an eclipse.**

Total Solar Eclipse (eclipse of sun)

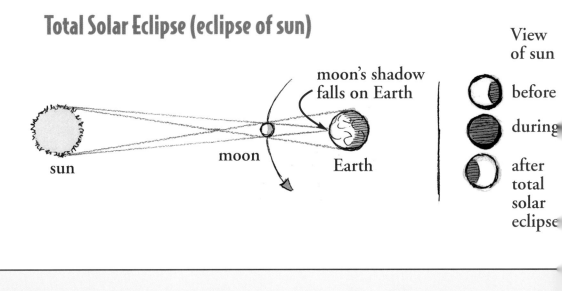

When Earth is directly between the sun and the moon, Earth's shadow falls on the moon. This is called a lunar eclipse, but the moon doesn't disappear. Some sunlight that is bent by Earth's air reaches the moon. This gives the moon a reddish color during a lunar eclipse. It is safe to observe lunar eclipses.

Total Lunar Eclipse (eclipse of moon)

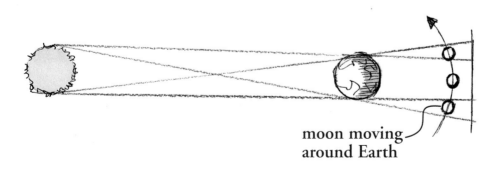

moon moving around Earth

Words to Know

lunar eclipse—A lunar eclipse happens when Earth is directly between the moon and the sun. Then Earth's shadow falls on the moon, and we see the moon grow dark.

meteoroids—Small objects moving through space that sometimes hit planets and moons. The moon's many craters were made by meteoroids that struck its surface.

midday—The time halfway between sunrise and sunset when the sun is highest in the sky.

new moon—A new moon is when the moon is between Earth and the sun. A new moon cannot be seen from Earth because all the sunlight hitting the moon is reflected away from Earth.

prism—A wedge-shaped piece of glass or plastic object that can bend light, separating white light into all the colors it contains.

rainbow—A semicircle of colors from red to violet made when sunlight is reflected and bent by raindrops. From an airplane you can sometimes see a full circle of colors.

shadow—An area where light is blocked by an object.

solar eclipse—A solar eclipse occurs when the moon is directly between Earth and the sun. Then the moon's shadow falls on Earth. Within the shadow, all or part of the sun is blocked from view.

Further Reading

Books

Bochinski, Julianne Blair. *The Complete Workbook for Science Fair Projects.* New York: John Wiley and Sons, 2004.

Branley, Franklyn M. *What the Moon Is Like.* New York: HarperCollins, 2000.

Dispezio, Michael A. *Super Sensational Science Fair Projects.* New York: Sterling Publishing, 2002.

Pipe, Jim. *Sun.* Mankato, Minn.: Stargazer Books, 2005.

Simon, Seymour. *The Moon.* New York: Simon & Schuster Books for Young Readers, 2003.

Tomecek, Steve. *Moon.* Washington, D.C.: National Geographic Society, 2004.

Internet Addresses

Arnett, Bill. *The Nine Planets.*
<http://www.nineplanets.org/sol.html>

NASA. *Star Child.* <http://www.nasa.gov>
Click on "For Kids," then "Star Child," then "Solar System" to learn more about the sun and moon.

Index